tredition®

AF597561

Publisher: tredition, Hamburg, Germany

978-3-7439-8924-5 (Paperback)
978-3-7439-8925-2 (Hardcover)

Printed on demand in many countries

ESL Activities for the Classroom

Natalie S. Johnson

TABLE OF CONTENTS

ACKNOWLEDGEMENTS

I would like to acknowledge all of the teachers in our programs, as well as the wonderful and enthusiastic students who practice their English in the schools in which I teach.

INTRODUCTION

Most of the activities in this book are at the level of an intermediate middle to high-school age ESL student. Some activities are appropriate for beginners, and others for more advanced students. The activities are compiled and presented for teachers of ESL who are familiar with the short-stay program format, and who know that students are often of mixed levels in the classrooms. If you find that your students are not able to perform a task, you can modify the activity to fit your needs, or move on to another.

These activities and materials do not align exactly with any specific standards of any specific learning community, school, or language teaching institution. The activities and materials are not curriculum for any public, or private institution granting diplomas or degrees.

PREFACE

All of the activities, handouts, and ideas in this book have been created by the author. The activities engage learners who are attending short-term programs. The activities utilize previously learned skills in English, as well as provide activities for learners in long-term classroom settings. The activities allow for practice in speaking and interacting in English, and for having fun in a classroom setting. The activities can be used internationally in a language classroom, and can be translated for use.

I created these activities after four years of teaching short-stay programs for students who visit the United States to study English, tour the area, and stay with local families. I like this book because now I do not have to search for teaching material for every program that I teach. Since the students are always new, the material never gets old for my classes. I can add to activities as I like, and I can modify to fit my students' needs and levels of proficiency.

There are many different ways to introduce students to their class, their new teachers, and to others. Introductory activities can also be used a few days into the class. They are a way for students to connect and make friends. These activities help teachers learn about their students. As the teacher, you are encouraged to walk around the room, mingle with your students, get engaged in some of the conversations, give a little feedback, and express interest in what the students have to say. This can often be the most favorable introduction you can give of yourself to the students. That's because this represents you as interested in the students and the class, and as an interesting person who has ideas about topics and who enjoys meeting people.

Activity #1

MAKING NAME TAGS AND FOLDERS

Materials: plain white paper or lined paper or stock paper, heavy duty, colored, large-sized paper or folders already made, markers, stickers, glue, glitter, stapler

Skills: collaboration, creativity, making friends while you work

After choosing a seating arrangement based upon your classroom space, teaching style, planned groupings, movements, and age of students, hand out some white or colored paper 8-1/2" x 11" and have the students fold this lengthwise. They then write their first name and decorate as they choose. You could also suggest that they add a picture of a sport or hobby, a favorite animal, or some other theme-related picture. Then, if you have time, you can make folders with large-sized colored paper and a stapler, or you can buy ready-made folders with pockets for students. They can spend a few minutes decorating their folders and talking about their first night in the new country while they work. This gives you a chance to work some more on setting up your classroom talking to the students directly, and previewing and learning their names.

Variation #1: Consider also having the students each complete an index card with their name on it and one interesting thing about themselves, you can use this as the teacher to learn about them.

Variation #2: Students can draw a picture to give to you to learn about them, or to exchange and read aloud or share.

Activity #2

ALL ABOUT ME

Materials: copies of the survey, pens or pencils *Skills: reading, writing, and speaking*

This self-survey works well in any kind of classroom, whether young children or adults. Students complete the survey and share with others. Variation #1: Complete this after a few days of class have gone by, leave the names off the handout, switch them around, read them aloud and try to guess who it is! Whoever gets the right name reads next.

SURVEY

Name ______________________ Class or teacher ____________________

I am ___________ years old. I live in _________________.

I have _____ brothers and sisters.

I have a pet. My pet's name is _______________. He/she is a _____________.

I go to ______________ school.

I am in _______________ grade.

My favorite teacher is ___________. My favorite subject is_______________.

My favorite game is_______________. My favorite food is ________________

I am staying with _________________________________ (family, friends).

Activity #3

SCAVENGER QUESTIONS

Materials: envelopes, slips of paper, questions on a handout, pens or pencils, prizes such as pencils and erasers or notepaper or stickers, a space to "hunt" in

Skills: reading, speaking listening, cooperation

If you are only able to use one room for your class, and the space that you are in doesn't allow you to navigate into the rest of a facility, you can consider going outside for your "hunt," or you can invent a way to do it inside.

Set paper lunch bags around the room in various locations. Number the bags. Next to the bags put slips of paper and pens. Each bag will correspond to a question on a given handout. The students circulate around the room, matching the station number on the bag with the corresponding question on their handout. They then go to the station, answer the question on the slip of paper and put it into the bag. When they have completed all of the questions, they get to the FINAL station, and get their prize. Questions may be: what is your favorite color, class, teacher, song, movie, book, etc. You can decide if you would like their name on the slip. You can collect these to learn more about the class.

Activity #4

SCAVENGER HUNT

Materials: map or directions, prizes, envelopes *Skills: directions, cooperation, listening, speaking*

Utilize a larger space and place envelopes in locations throughout the space. Give the students a "Scavenger Hunt map" with the locations listed on it. They must follow the map to get the clue to go to the next location. Here is where you can get creative. You can hide pieces of a puzzle in envelopes that they must put together at the end to get their prizes, or you can have them each pick up a number, a colored paper or a sticker to provide proof of having participated to get their prize at the end. You can identify the locations by a physical object that you have placed the clue on or next to. For example: find envelope #13 taped to the lamp on the table by the front door; or you can utilize the opportunity to have them actually follow specific directions (for example: go up the stairs, turn right, walk to first door on the right, turn right, go straight, etc.).

Activity #5

CONVERSATION SCAVENGER HUNT

I used this at a college campus visit with my students. I gave the students a list of instructions to engage in conversation with people on the campus. The students had to ask people to take their picture, to give them directions to a certain location, to tell them the price of something (in the bookstore), to ask them for the best restaurant, where to park their car, where the bus stop is, etc. They had to check off this list as they went through it in small groups. I think that they had a good time with this one.

Activity #6

GREETINGS and HAND SHAKES

Materials: Handouts, pencils

Skills: speaking and listening, asking questions, circulating and trying out new skills

In the U.S people usually shake hands when meeting. This symbolizes trust. People do some "small talk" and ask each other questions to keep the conversation going. This means that they will ask a question or two that is *easy to answer*.

The following is an activity to practice this American custom. Be sure to model this, perhaps with a volunteer student.

Script below:

Students A and B.

A: Hello. My name is _________________. I am a student from _______.

B: Nice to meet you. My name is ___________. I am a student from _______ (or a teacher, or a parent, etc).

A: Nice to meet you.

Question: How was the flight over?

B: ***Answer:*** ____________________________________.

Question: *Did anything interesting happen on your flight over?*

A: ***Answer:*** ____________________________________.

Question: *How long will you be staying?*

B: ***Answer:*** ____________________________________.

A: ***Question:*** ?

Below are some additional questions for this type of introductory conversation.

"How do you like the US so far?" "Is the weather a lot different?" "Do you think people are friendly here?" "Have you been to the US before?" "What other countries have you visited?" "What is one thing you would like to do while you are in the US?" Keep it topic-specific.

Activity #7

INTEREST SURVEYS

Interest surveys are a great way for students to learn about each other, and for the teacher to learn about the students. From this information, you can design further conversations and activities to fit your specific class. They can be used as icebreakers, or ways to learn more about each other. Teachers can use them to develop topics for discussion or to locate sources for teaching such as music or books or articles that relate closely to the students' interests.

Continued next page.

Materials: Survey, pens or pencils *Skills: speaking, listening, writing* Handout:

What are some of your interests? List your name first, then ask four other students.

Student Name - Ask 4 Students ↓	Favorite Song and Group	Favorite Food	Favorite Sport *to watch or play*
(your name goes here)			
List who has the same song, food or sport here →			

Variation #1: Questions you could ask: "Have you been to a concert of your favorite music group?" "Where do you usually eat your favorite food?" "Do you like to cook?" "Do you play a sport, or just watch?"

Variation #2: Think of more questions that you can ask each other. When the teacher says "New Partners," change to a new partner and practice again. Share some of your questions with the class. Practice introducing someone to another student.

Teacher's note: Monitor the students closely and guide students through the activity, suggesting questions for them to ask.

Activity #8

ADVANCED SURVEY

Materials: Survey, pencils, Venn diagram *Skills: speaking, listening, writing,*

Handout: *Advanced Survey* with writing task.

Directions: Interview five people. Ask them to answer the five topics.					
Name	Topic 1	Topic 2	Topic 3	Topic 4	Topic 5
Your name here ________	Favorite Music	Favorite Movie	Favorite Food	Favorite Sport	Favorite Subject in School
Name ________					
Name ________					
Name ________					
Name ________					
Name ________					

Advanced survey continued…

Next: Choose a friend from your survey. In the center circle, write one topic that you and your friend both like. Then, pick a category that you don't share, and put one in the left circle and one in the right circle.

Then write three sentences about you and your friend.

Your Name _____________ Friend here_____________

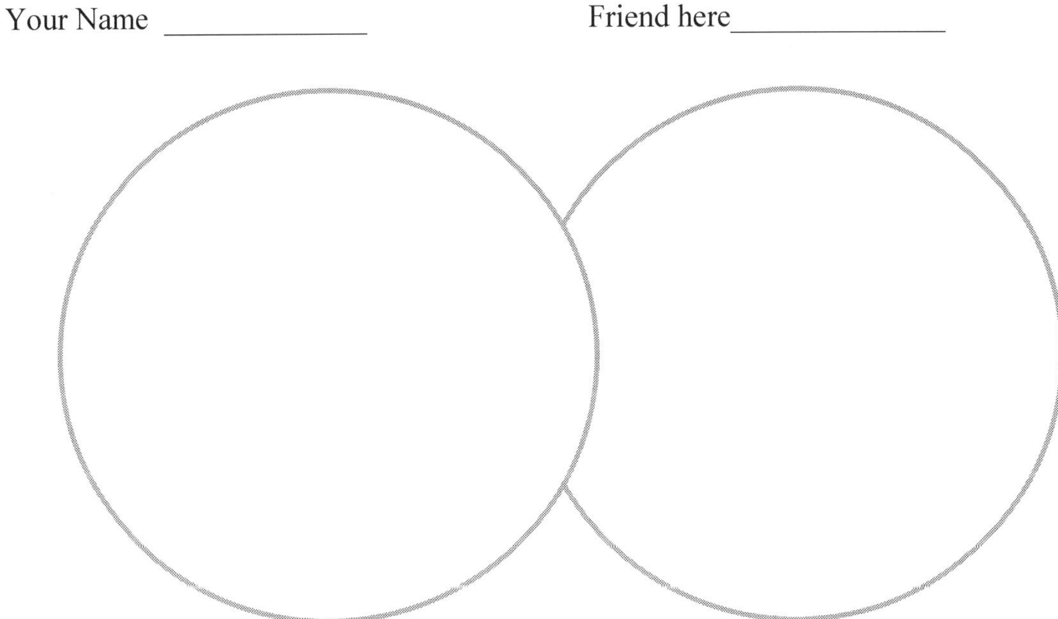

When preparing this, I suggest use of a Venn Diagram.

Write three sentences about you and your friend. Examples: Hana and I both like to listen to rock music. Hana likes her teacher Mr. Smith for English class. I like my teacher Ms. Johnson for English class.

1.

2.

3.

Activity #9

FIND SOMEONE WHO: BINGO CARD CHECK OFF

Materials: bingo cards, pens or pencils *Skills: speaking, listening, vocabulary*

This is a variation of the survey or "getting to know you" kinds of activities. I usually incorporate this after we have done a few different types of activities about what we like to do, such as: what our talents are and other ways to learn about each other in class, especially with beginners.

Directions: You are to find someone who has or does what is in each box. When you find someone, write their name in the box, then go on to find the next person who………

Has an older brother or sister Name:	Can speak another language (other than English) Name:	Doesn't like chocolate Name:	Knows how to ski (water or snow) Name:
Lives in the same city as his or her grandparents Name:	Has been to Europe Name:	Likes to wear hats Name:	Can drive a car Name:
Has a cat or a dog Name:	Plays a musical instrument Name:	Sings in the shower Name:	Can sew by hand or with a sewing machine Name:
Is learning how to program a computer Name:	Likes to cook <u>and</u> wash the dishes Name:	Has ever colored his or her hair Name:	Would like to attend college in the United States Name:

Activity #10

CHALLENGE STATIONS

Materials: handout, pens or pencils

Skills: speaking, listening, reading, interacting/kinesthetic

Directions: Ask someone if they can do these activities:

1. Can you say the alphabet in 15 seconds?

Who? ___________ can can't *(Name and circle one)*

2. Can you draw a square with one hand and a circle with the other hand?

Who? ___________ can can't

3. Can you tap your right foot and wave your left hand at the same time?

Who? ___________ can can't

4. Say this tongue twister:

Who? ___________ can can't

"Take time to talk. Yes, talking takes time, today. Texting on the telephone takes time, too. Taking time to talk to tell the things you need to do sometimes takes too much time. For example, it takes 10 to 20 minutes to tell a story to someone while texting or talking, which is twice the time it takes to try to do it."

Or this one….

"Could the cute kitten climb the cactus quickly? Or, did the kitty cry and meow quite loudly because she couldn't?"

Who? ___________ can can't

5. Can you say the months of the year backwards?

Who? ___________ can can't

Continued next page….

6. Can you say the days of the week backwards?

Who? ___________ can can't

7. Name the five senses:

Who? ___________ can can't

8. Can you fold an origami crane? Paper provided. (*optional)*

Who? ___________ can can't

Teacher's Note: Use the opportunity to talk about the activity. What was easy? What was hard?

Activity #11

INTRO BALL TOSS

Materials: inflated ball

Skills: Speaking and listening, generating questions, real-world connections

Select a topic of interest. I suggest this question: *"What have you noticed that is different here than where you are from?"* Some examples of differences might be: food, friendly or not friendly people, the weather, traffic lights, traffic patterns, money, etc. Start by tossing an inflated ball to one student and calling out his or her name. After they answer and give details, they toss the ball to another student who shares his or her name and answers the same question.

Variation #1: Have the first student come up with a new question, such as: "*What is your favorite hobby, class in school, what did you do this weekend, etc.?"*

Activity #12

INTRODUCTION TO NEW FRIENDS

Materials: board or poster with the words "Learn 3 things about someone" written on it, notecards, pens or pencils

Skills: Speaking and listening, generating questions, remembering details

Students are encouraged to pair up with someone whom they do not know yet, or don't know very well. Before you do so, however, brainstorm some good questions to get to know someone. Examples: grade, school, city from, languages spoken, favorite food, book or color, family, pets, travel plans, favorite vacation, or. Students must learn three things about their new friend. After 5 – 10 minutes of talking time, stop the class and nominate pairs to tell about each other.

Teacher's note: This activity is a good chance to circulate and do some informal assessment of speaking skills to guide planning of activities and lessons, give some reminders to speak in English, or help with pronunciation and grammar.

Activity #13

SPORTS POSTER

Materials: list of sports, questionnaire handout *Skills*: *Speaking, writing, listening,*

This is a good introduction activity for beginners. They can also learn who they may have something in common with in the classroom. Students interview as many people as possible in five minutes. While interviewing they write student names next to the sports that he or she plays. When done interviewing people, they report the most common sport played to the class. This can be extended into conversation about sports, lessons, teams, or a writing task about the sport or about learning to do something that you enjoy. I used this opportunity to discuss sports vocabulary words in English, and the students mimed the actions to go with the vocabulary.

Continued list on next page.

Soccer

Swimming

Bicycle riding

Tennis

Volleyball

Hockey

Ping Pong

Running/jogging

Karate/Martial Arts

Horseback riding

Games and skits are great ways to practice language through activities that are fun, engaging and challenging. Be flexible and let everyone find his or her comfort zone. Especially with younger students and short-stay programs, it isn't necessary to stress over non-participation of part of any activity in the classroom

Moving around is a good way for students to relax and wake up, also. Sometimes these kinds of games are good for an icebreaker, or for a rainy day.

MOVEMENT and ACTION!

ACTIVE ***Get-To-Know-You-Games***

Activity #14

THE HUMAN KNOT

Materials: none *Skills: cooperation, speaking, listening*

Students form a circle, cross their hands and grab onto the hands of someone else in the circle, but not the person next to them. They then have to twist and turn to unknot themselves into a normal circle of people holding hands. A smaller circle usually works best.

Activity #15

EGG ON THE SPOON or BEAN BAG ON THE HEAD

Materials: plastic or metal spoon, boiled egg or ping-pong ball and/or beanbags

Skills: teamwork, collaboration, active

There are many variations of this kind of an icebreaker game. Teams form lines and walk from the start of the line to a tape or spot on the floor and back again without dropping the spoon or allowing the beanbag to fall off their head. If the entire team does this without dropping the object and/or they are finished first, they win.

Activity #16

IT'S A GREAT DAY FOR....

Materials: chairs or squares on the floor *Skills: cooperation, listening, speaking*

Here the students sit in a circle on chairs or on a tape X on the floor. There is one less spot than number of students. The first student stands in the middle, selects an article of clothing and says: "Today is a great day for people wearing (for example) tennis shoes." Then everyone who is wearing tennis shoes has to get up and select a new spot. Whoever is left without a seat is the next speaker in the middle. This works better in smaller groups to discourage running.

Activity #17

FIVE SKITS

Materials: Skit readings printed for student use (you can certainly write your own, and include pictures if you'd like) *Skills: reading, acting, cooperation, listening*

Most students actually like to do some acting. Many English learners are motivated to learn English because it is fun to do. This just adds to the fun. A collaborative writing and acting extension of this activity would be for students to team up and either write or improvise a skit of their own to act out. Additional ideas are to hand out scripts from traditional fairy tales from any country, and then ask students to put together a fairy tale from their own cultures either in written or acted format.

This is similar to a Readers Theater format, but much shorter. Encourage a round of applause and maybe even an encore!

Skit #1 - Three students deciding what movie to go to.

Students are A, B, and C.

A: Hi there! What are you going to do after class today?

B: We are just talking about that right now. We can't decide what we want to do.

C: Right. I think it would be fun to just go to my house.

A: What movie do you want to see?

B: Captain America. I heard that it is very good.

C: And I heard that it is boring!

A: Awww, come on....it can't be that bad. Little kids go to that movie!

C: Well, I still might not like it.

A: We should go. I don't think it will be bad.

C: Ok, but if I fall asleep when I am watching the movie, it will be your fault!

A: OK, but you won't fall asleep. You will like the movie.

B: I don't know if you will like it that much.

A: Can we go to the one that starts at 5:30? I need to do my homework.

C: I have homework, too.

B: Ok. Let's go right now. We can get popcorn at the movie.

Skit #2 - Two students talking about shopping

Student A and B

A: I got some new shoes and a new jacket this weekend. I really needed new clothes.

B: Did you get clothes for school?

A: Yeah. And, I got ski boots and some gloves, too.

B: Really? Where did you go shopping?

A: I went with my mom to REI.

B: Lucky you! That place is really expensive.

A: It wasn't bad.

B: You must be kidding?

A: Yeah. My mom paid for it!

B: OK. So it was not expensive for you, but it was for her.

A: Yes.

B: Can I go shopping with you?

Skit #3 - Three students deciding where to eat.

Students are A, B, and C and D.

A; I am hungry.

B: So am I.

C: I can wait, I guess.

D: I feel like eating ice cream, and French fries and burgers.

B: Not me. Where should we go to eat?

C: I think pizza would be good.

A: I would like to eat spaghetti with meatballs and bread.

B: Both sound good.

D: A chocolate milk shake sounds good. And ice cream with fudge and cherries on it.

A: There is a really good Italian restaurant just a few blocks away. We can walk there.

C: What about the pizza place that is right across the street? See it? Pizza Palace.

A: Pizza Palace has really good pizza.

B: Yes, it does.

C: So, we should go there, right?

Continued.

A: The Italian restaurant has pizza and spaghetti. We could eat there and we would all get what we want to eat.

D: Do they have ice cream?

A: Yes, but they don't have French fries.

B: Ok. That is a really good idea.

C: I agree. Italian it is.

D: Ok.

Skit #4 - Three students talking about school uniforms. Students are A, B and C.

A: Hi guys! How are you?

B and C: (Together) OK, How are you?

A: I am ok. Except I don't want to wear a school uniform any more. I like t-shirts with logos.

B: I see. Like the t-shirts and jeans that you wear all summer?

C: And every weekend?

A: Yes. The shirts I wear have things I like on them. I don't have to say anything. The shirt shows what I like.

B: That is true. Our school clothes don't tell much about us. They are all the same.

C: Yes, but it sure is easy to get dressed in the morning.

A: But I want to decide what to wear.

B: To school.

C: Yes, to school and everywhere, right?

A: Yes. We should get students to say that they want to wear cool clothes to school.

B: Maybe. But I know my parents like the uniforms.

C: My parents like the uniforms. I don't see anything wrong with wearing them.

A: It is ok, I guess. I always look the same, so that is the good thing.

B: Get a different haircut. Color your hair.

A: That would be something new.

C: Go for it!

A: Maybe I will.

Skit #5 – Two students talking about a test. They think that they got good grades. They want to ask the teacher, but decide to wait. Students are A and B.

A: That was a really hard test we had in class today!

B: I think I got a good grade.

A: I think I did, too.

B: What should we do?

A: Are you going to tell your parents before you know your grade?

B: No. Probably not. Why does the teacher give such hard tests? But I did study. So I did well.

A: I want to know my grade. I think I have another test tomorrow.

B: Let's go talk to the teacher.

A: OK. We can ask about our grades.

B: I want to talk to her now.

A: If she says to wait until tomorrow to ask, we will have to wait.

B: I won't sleep tonight.

A: I am not worried. I think I will wait until tomorrow.

Teacher's note: Follow each performance with applause.

Variations #1: Ask the students if they want to perform theirs again.

Variation #2: Offer to allow video recording with cell phones.

Variation #3: Have the class vote for the best group or skit.

Activity #18

JIGSAW CLUES AND POINTERS

This game is similar to a familiar game show, but with the added twist of a jigsaw activity, where groups of students on each team have clues for the players, who then "use up" their "points" each time that they access a clue from the other team. The challenge for the teacher is to have the categories and clues well-matched, and to keep score in a visible location.

Materials: Board or poster paper with four categories: for example: American holidays, travel sites around the world, food, sports, names of American school courses, famous musicians, film, movie stars, computer games. (Make sure that, for a class of 15-20 students, you have five topic categories, four subcategories, and three clues for each of the four subcategories.) Also be prepared with the clues listed by point value. You may need a score keeper, a referee, and a timer if players are taking too long.

Skills: speaking, reading, remembering facts, teamwork and cooperation

Post the categories on the board or poster paper. Under each category, list: 400, 300, 200, 100 in a column. These are the points that the student will receive on each consecutive attempt at an answer, decreasing the number of points with each "clue" he or she requests. Divide the class into two teams. Have the team that is giving clues divide up the clues you have prepared by topic sub-category.

Jigsaw continued…

Example One: Category topic is American Holidays. (The subcategory is the holiday: The Fourth of July). The first clue (which you have provided to the opposing team in writing) is read to the student by the opposing team. If the student answers the category correctly with this clue, the team gets 400 points. If not, the student then asks for the second clue. If they answer the category correctly after this clue is provided, the team gets 300 points.

Some clues for American Holidays might be: 400 points: celebration with fireworks, flags, and picnics; 300 points: occurs in the middle of summer; 200 points: marks the independence of the U.S. from Britain; 100 points: *student was not able to answer, but he or she did try!*

Other topic categories: Money, Oceans of the World, Food, Sports, Careers.

Example 2: Let's do Money as a Topic Category: Four subcategories might be: five dollar bill, dime, quarter, dollar amount of largest U.S. bill. The student who is playing for points selects one of these subcategories. Then he or she chooses how many points she or he would like to earn for the team that they are on and asks the opposing team for information that is a clue with that point value associated to it. Clues for a five dollar bill would be: 400 points: has President Lincoln on it; 300 points: is made of paper; 200 points: 4 of these make $20.00, 100 points: student not able to answer.

Teacher's note: Try to have a tie-breaker question ready for the very end that you allow the students from each team to work on together. Make the value of this much larger so that a definite winner is obvious. Monitor closely throughout the game to make sure everyone gets a chance to answer a category. This requires knowledge of how many students you will be teaching in order to prepare enough categories and clues.

Activity #19

WHAT IS THE BAG?

Materials: paper lunch bags, stickers, various small objects that fit into the bags

Skills: *movement, use of English, visualizing*

Practice describing an object and what it's used for, without using the name of the item when speaking.

Give each student a paper bag with an item in it. Tell them not to let anyone see what is in their bag before giving it to them. Items may be such things as: rubber bands, paper clips, a postage stamp, a quarter, an old or fake credit card, a bus pass, a bus schedule, a movie ticket, a receipt, a crayon, etc.

Model this activity first: Example clues

Paper clip: holds papers together, made of metal, bent in shape
Rubber band: stretchy, holds papers together, round in shape
Stamp: used for mailing letters, goes on an envelope, used to send letters

Include 3-4 fun stickers in the bag. Students circulate and try to get up to 3-4 people to guess what is in their bag. A correct guess gets a sticker. The person with the most stickers after 5-10 minutes go by wins.

Activity #20

ROOMS IN THE HOUSE

Materials: Large poster paper pieces or sections of a black or white board, markers, list of items found in a typical home or apartment for each student, strips of room names to pick

Skills: *reading, speaking, listening, action, teamwork*

Give each student a list of typical household and garage/garden items Read the list or have them read it silently.

Let them know that they will be playing a game using the words but that they have to study the vocabulary first. Put up a poster of the rooms in a house (garage is optional) in large print at the front of the room. Divide the students into two teams. Give the first in line a marker. Select room name strips without looking from a hat or cup. At the reading of each room name, the students go to their board and write an item from the list that used in that room.

Variation #1: Put the items on colored sticky notes next to the poster or board and have the students move the sticky note item that goes with the room that has been read out loud. Whichever team has the most correct words for each room wins.

Continued next page.

Variation #2: Set up one poster, give two teams each a marker, and read an item from the list one for one team, one for the next. They put a team-colored "X" on the poster for the room in which the item is usually found.

Variation #3: Divide into two teams. Set up 1-2 posters. Hand out a sticky or markers to "X." Then read from a list of statements such as: "I need to make popcorn," or, "I need to wash the dishes but I don't a lot of time," or, "I need to put the milk away," "I want to brush my teeth." The students then go to the poster/board and mark or move the sticky note to the correct room.

Activity #21

BODY PARTS FOR BEGINNERS

Materials: Two large posters of an outline of a human body, sticky notes with body parts written on them such as: elbow, knee, chin, nose, eyes, ear, mouth, ankle, stomach, head, neck, etc. markers.

Skills: reading, listening, cooperation and team work

Line up two teams. Designate speaker/reader and the scorekeeper. Usually this would be the teacher. You can name your poster guy/gal with a fictitious name to make it more fun. Then read off the following types of statements one at a time: "My _____ hurts."

Body parts continued.

The students run to their poster and put an “X” on the body part that they heard you say, one from each team at a time per body part read. Move the sticky note with the body part on it to the correct location on the poster person. If it is right, the team gets a point. This can be really fun and a good laugh when someone gets the wrong part!

Teacher’s note This activity is good for beginner learners, as they may need reminders on how to tell someone that they don’t feel well, and what body part is affected. A variation would be to pass the “My ____ hurts” statement through the line from the back to the front player and see if it has translated correctly.

Teacher’s note: This is not a Simon Says game! Do not include that in this activity, as it will likely confuse the students. They are to practice speaking and following through with directions, as well as visual and kinesthetic learning that connects with what they are listening for.

If you are concerned that students don’t know all of their body parts English names, you could sing that popular “head, shoulders, etc.” song from nursery school……

Activity #22

PROFESSIONS GAME

Materials: list of professions by name, scissors, envelopes *Skills: reading, listening,*

In this game, each student gets one half of a profession/job description matching activity. They circulate around the room and find the matching profession/job description, and then wait to share reading it out to the class in pairs. The lists below are cut into slips and handed out.

Doctor	Dentist
Mechanic	Computer technician
Veterinarian	Teacher
Bus driver	Lawyer
Astronaut	Scientist
Athlete	Chef
Pilot	Hair Stylist or a barber

Professions continued…

A ____________________ checks your health, fixes broken bones, and operates.

A ____________________ fixes broken teeth and cavities.

A ____________________ fixes your car.

A _____________________ checks your pet's health.

A ___________________ helps students learn subjects in school.

A ___________________ drives students to school and other places.

A ___________________ helps people with the law in court cases.

A ___________________ goes into outer space to learn about space science.

A ____________________ experiments in a lab and invents discovers science facts.

An ______________________ plays professional sports.

A ______________________ creates and runs programs and software.

A _______________________ cooks food in a restaurant.

A _____________________________ flies people around the world in an airplane.

A _______________________ cuts peoples hair.

Teacher's note: This one is actually good as the mix matches can be funny.

Activity #23

BASEBALL

Materials: notecards with questions, markers for bases and pitcher's mound, referee

Skills: Cooperation and teamwork, speaking, listening, responding, physical movement

In Seattle, as in many places, baseball is a popular American sport. It is also played around the globe. The following game is based upon a baseball game format. The pitcher pitches the questions, and the players on each team have a chance to answer correctly and take a base, or strike out and sit on the bench until the next round. The questions can be adjusted according to topic, age or level of proficiency, or interests. For a variation, have the teams make up questions for the other team to answer. Just make sure that there are enough to go around at least once.

Below are some sample questions.

Questions for baseball

How many syllables are in the word dic-tion-ar-y

ANSWER:

4

Name three fruits that are red:

ANSWER:

apple, cherry, strawberry, plum, raspberry,

Name 3 foods that are green

ANSWER:

lettuce, beans, peas, spinach, apples, limes, mint, cabbage, olives, peppers

---

I like pizza. Ask me a question about pizza.

ANSWER:

You decide if the question is a good one.

Use this adjective in a sentence about a delicious food:

"tasty"

ANSWER: (…)

Check with teacher if necessary.

Make this word plural and spell it"

"butterfly"

ANSWER:

"b-u-t-t-e-r-f-l-i-e-s"

Make this word plural and spell it"

"hobby"

ANSWER:

Hobbies

I play tennis.

Say this sentence in the past tense.

ANSWER:

I played tennis.

What's missing from this sequence?

1st, 2nd, 3rd, 4th, 6th, 7th, 8th, 9th, 10th

ANSWER:

5th

Do you say:

"an apple", or "a apple"

Ask me if I would like to eat one.

ANSWER:

Would you like to eat an apple?

What are the five vowels in the English language?

ANSWER:

a, e, I, o, u

Name the four seasons in the calendar year.

ANSWER:

Spring, summer, winter, fall (or autumn)

How many letters are in the English alphabet?

ANSWER:

26

I have a pet at home. He has long hair, pointy ears,

And likes to chase birds. What is he?

ANSWER:

A cat

What does this saying mean:

"as light as a feather"

ANSWER:

Something that weighs about the same as a feather

What is the opposite word for:

Better

ANSWER:

Worse

There are two different ways to spell the word "here" (hear)

What are they? Hint: you can say "hear" and signal your ear, and "here" and point to where you are

ANSWER:

Hear and here

What is the contraction (or ANOTHER WAY TO SAY…) for

"I will"

ANSWER:

I'll

Which side of the road do people drive on in the UK?

ANSWER:

The left

Name three nouns that have something to do with school:

ANSWER:

Teacher, students, desks, books, computers, chairs, food, paper, pencils

---

Change this sentence to the past tense:

"I like the birthday party."

ANSWER:

I liked the birthday party.

Change this sentence to the present tense.

"I liked reading about bike races."

ANSWER:

"I like reading about bike races."

Name three toppings that people put on ice cream.

ANSWER:

Chocolate, strawberries, butterscotch, nuts, sprinkles, cherries, bananas, whipped cream

---

Name five things that you can do at a library:

ANSWER:

Check out a book, make copies, print pages, use the computer, study, read a book, read a magazine, meet people, check out music or a movie

---

Make this word into a noun:

"musical" As in "The woman singing is very musical." She likes to sing………

ANSWER:

"music"

Make this word into an adjective (A describing word):

"color"

ANSWER:

"colorful"

Spell the following word

Baseball

ANSWER:

B a s e b a l l

What do you call your mother's brother in English?

ANSWER:

Your uncle

How many states are there in the United States?

ANSWER:

50

Are American banks open on Sundays?

ANSWER:

No

Can I buy a computer in most American grocery stores?

ANSWER:

No.

What word describes the teacher in this sentence?

"He has a nice teacher."

ANSWER:

nice

Spell the word "letter" as in "mail a letter…."

ANSWER:

"l-e-t-t-e-r"

What should say to someone who gives you a compliment?

ANSWER:

"Thank you."

How many pennies are in one dollar"

ANSWER:

100

How many people are there on a baseball team?

ANSWER:

9

How many bases are there on a baseball field?

ANSWER:

4 (count the home plate)

How many people are there on a soccer team?

ANSWER:

7-11

How many people are there on a basketball team?

ANSWER:

5

What sport is played on a court with 2 or 4 players, a green ball and racquets?

ANSWER:

Tennis

What sport is played on ice?

ANSWER:

Hockey

What does a referee do?

ANSWER:

Makes sure the game is played fairly. Tells people when they do something wrong.

What are the names of the U.S. coins that make up a dollar?

ANSWER:

Quarter, dime, nickel and penny

Americans have a holiday in December when people put a tree in the house and decorate it, give presents and have a holiday meal. What is this holiday?

ANSWER:

Christmas

How many year do Americans go to school in order to graduate and go to college?

ANSWER:

12

Seattle, Washington is on the west coast next to the Pacific Ocean. What is the name of the ocean that borders the east coast of the United States?

ANSWER:

The Pacific Ocean

What famous children's game was originated by a Japanese man, and quickly caught on in the U.S., with games, trading cards, and a series on TV?

ANSWER:

Pokemon

What is the language spoken by most Canadians?

ANSWER:

English

Other than English, what language is spoken in Canada?

ANSWER:

French

Name the seven days of the week in order starting with Monday.

ANSWER:

Monday, Tuesday, Wednesday, Thursday, Friday, Saturday, Sunday

---

Name at least three pets that someone might have in their apartment.

ANSWER:

Cat, dog, bird, fish, snake, rat, mouse, hamster, Iguana, spiders

---

A bag that you can put your books in and carry on your back is called a…..

ANSWER:

Backpack

The bag that women carry and put things in is called a:

ANSWER: Purse

What time is it if it is “Noon”?

ANSWER: 12 pm

Activity #24

BLINDFOLD ACTIVITIES

Materials: blindfolds, sticky notes, space to move safely with guidance and no vision.

Skills: Giving directions, understanding directions, cooperation, assisting someone.

Blindfold activities are a great way to practice giving and getting directions. Students seem to really like these and there is a lot of laughter and fun. Team students into pairs, where one gives the directions and the other tries to follow with a blindfold on. Then they switch. Be wise to dangerous areas, or stairs or outside activities that might cause injury.

Variation #1:Blindfold student A. Give the sighted student B a sticky note on which they write their names. Tell student B to place the sticky note somewhere in the room, or hallway. Then they must direct student B to the note. At that point, they can switch and go back or to another location. The prize is in the fun, and who gets done first!

Activity #25

RESTAURANT

Materials: Table, chairs, place settings, menus from local restaurants, script, waiter's pad and pencil. *Skills*: *Reading a menu, speaking or placing an order, listening, writing*

Find a local restaurant that will give you a menu to make copies from or find one online. Seat the students at tables. Prepare a script similar to the following. Designate a waiter. The tableware can be pretend or real.

Have the students follow the script at first. They will probably have fun with this. Eventually they won't need a script, and can improvise.

Variation #1: add items to the menu in pencil, or make up favorite food items; complain; pay the bill with play money for practice; spill food.

Variation #2: You may also want to have a volunteer "couple" and waiter or one person and waiter to model the activity first.

You can write your own menu. The one I prepared looks like this:

<u>Menu</u>

<u>Entrees</u>:

Spaghetti with or without meatballs, meatballs $1.00 extra

Pizza – cheese, pepperoni or sausage or combo, combo is $3.00 extra

Steak and potatoes – fries, baked, mashed potato

Hot dogs and fries

Cheeseburger or hamburger and fries

Sides:

Fries

Salad

Soup of the day

Dessert:

Cake of the day

Ice cream – vanilla, chocolate or strawberry

Yogurt

Drinks:

Pop – regular or diet

Coffee or tea, hot or iced

Student Script

Actors include: Patrons A, B, C and D, Waiter, Chef

For a script: you could model yours after the following script, or you could do a short model activity with some students, then divide the class into groups and have them create a play or improvise as they go. Have them perform for each other.

Waiter: Welcome to our restaurant. I will be your waiter today. Here are your menus. I will return to take your orders.

A: "Thank you."

B: "What should we order? "

C: "Let's order our own food and pay for it ourselves."

D. "Sounds good."

Waiter returns: "May I take your order?"

(Students can improvise here, but be sure that they are using English).

A – D place their orders. Here they can be asked or give some choices from the menu. The waiter can return to the kitchen to ask the chef what the soup of the day is, or the cake of the day. The patrons can complain, the waiter can mix up the orders, the patrons can spill or the waiter can spill. They can ask to speak to the chef, refuse to leave a tip, and more.

Activity #26

CAKE ACTIVITY

Materials: ingredients for the cake listed below on slips of paper, tables for each group of 3-4 students. *Skills: teamwork, speaking, listening, kinesthetic*

Handout the "Ingredients for the Cake" as follows:

Your team needs: (You need enough of these slips for each team to have this list).

Salt – 2 teaspoons

Eggs - 4

Flour – 3 cups

Sugar – 2 cups

Milk – 2 cups

Butter – 2 cups

Chocolate - 2 cups

Your team only has:

Salt – 1 teaspoon

Eggs – 3

Flour – 2 cups

Sugar – 1 cups

Milk - 1 cup

Butter – 1 cup

Chocolate – 1 cup

Directions: Send one person out to Rock/paper/scissors win each ingredient, one at a time, only one from a team, then must bring the item back to your team, and go get something else that you need. It is up to you how your team will organize the items on your table. The first team to get all of the ingredients yells "Cake" and wins.

Students will send out a player to other team tables and play rock/paper/scissors with one of the other team's players. If they win, they and pick an ingredient, and bring it back to the table. Then that team decides what else they need and goes out to get it and bring it back.

There are seven different ingredients, seven teams and one umpire. He or she (or the teacher) will decide winners of rock/paper/scissors, watch for cheating, and make sure people do not run into each other. If there is a tie on the rock/paper/scissors game play, the player must go on to the next person, if the "taker of ingredients" loses, they go on to the next "team."

Activity #27

MIME/CHARADES Materials:List of mime actions *Skills: kinesthetic, connections, expression*

Cut these actions into separate slips, put into a bag or a hat, and have students draw out what they will do. Give them a few minutes to prepare, but they cannot talk to each other before or while they are acting! This is great for an ice breaker, say the second or third day, and works well as an introduction to verbs and the continuous tense.

Eat an apple	Laugh at a funny joke
Paint a picture of someone	Sharpen a pencil
Bowling	Swimming
Buy popcorn and watch a movie	Wrap a present
Grocery shop with a cart and put things into the cart from the shelves	Watch a funny movie and eat pop-corn.
Make a pizza	Walk a dog

Play pool	Play tennis
Send a text message on a cell phone	Wash dishes
Brush your teeth	Take someone's picture. Ask them to pose and smile.

Activity #28

DESCRIBING FOOD

Materials: handout

Skills: reading, writing, discussion, independent work

Food is a good concept to use vocabulary about the five senses. For a short-stay program, this gives the students the opportunity to practice and learn some new words to talk about food. Since they may be new to the country, they will likely try some new foods and might be asked what they think of it!

Use the handout below to work on some vocabulary related to the senses.

Five Senses Handout

Name: ________________________________ Date: _______________

People have five senses: *see, hear, smell, taste and touch*

These senses help us to experience and feel the world around us in many ways.

For example: What is your *favorite food*?

____

Directions: pick words from the word bank below to describe your favorite food.

See: ____

Hear: ____

Smell: ____

Taste: ____

Touch: ____

Word bank is continued on the next page.

Five Senses Word Bank

See size or shape or color	**Hear** When you make or eat it:	**Smell**	**Taste**	**Touch**
large or small	crunchy	spicy	hot and spicy	gooey
color:red, green,yel-low, orange, purple, blue, brown	pop	sweet	sweet	hot
round	fizz	choco-laty	sour	sticky
triangle	slurp	fruity	salty	soft
square	chewy	meaty	juicy	hard
long	smushy	fishy	fishy	cold
short	bubble	stinky	fruity	creamy

Activity #29

DESCRIBING FOOD ITEMS - BEGINNERS

Materials: List of the five senses, small poster paper or plain white paper, markers, colored pencils.

Skills: imagination, fluency, speaking, making connections

Discuss the five senses, perhaps using pictures as examples, or you can act out experiencing the five senses with relation to an example of a food item.

You may want to provide a list of adjectives to use first if your students are beginners. Some examples are: colors, such as red, orange; textures, such as smooth, bumpy; tastes, such as salty, sour, spicy; size, such as big or small; shapes, such as circle or round, or triangle (like a slice of pizza); specific flavors, such as cheesy, chocolate, nuts, vanilla, cinnamon. Examples would be words to describe the food item's color and shape, texture, smell, taste, sound when making and/or eating the item, or even the country of its origin or if it is a meat, vegetable, drink or desert.

Handout some paper and markers and colored pencils. Have the students select a food that they like, draw it and write as many describing words as they can think of around their picture.

Discussions and debates give students a chance to practice their English in pairs or in groups. They can express opinions, use code switching from L1 to English and back, and help each other with ideas and vocabulary. It is a good idea to explain to your students what a debate is. Your students may have participated in a debate or a similar activity in their home schools.

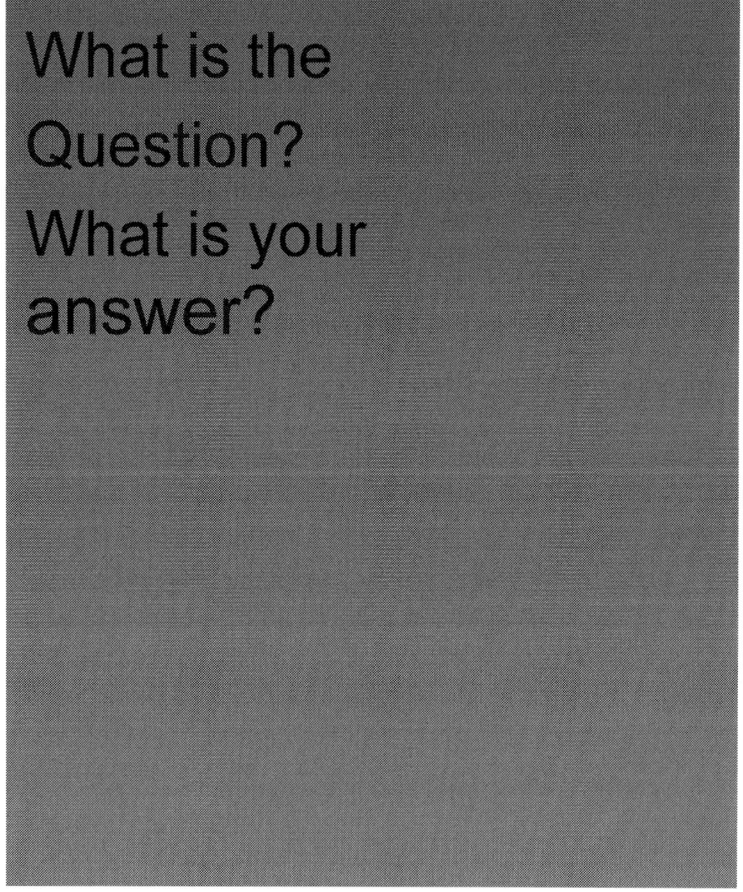

Activity #30

TWO-MINUTE DEBATES

Materials: list of topics, timer *Skills: listening, speaking*

Debate concept and choice topics. Explain to your students what a debate is. Likely, they have done a debate or a similar activity in their home schools.

Divide into two teams. Students face each other and debate/discuss as timed for two minutes. One side will be for and the other against. After 2 minutes, the line shifts and the students move on to another partner. You will announce a different topic. Make sure they understand that one side if the "for" side, and the other is the "against" or opposite/opposing side.

Example Topic: Ice Cream is good for you.

For:

1. There is milk in ice cream and milk is good for you.
2. It is ok to eat some sweets every day.
3. There are many kinds of delicious and healthy toppings, like bananas, cherries, and nuts.
4. Eating ice cream is social, so it is a good thing to do with other people.
5. Ice cream is not very expensive.
6. Everyone likes ice cream.
7. Ice cream goes good with cake, cookies, pies and other desserts.
8. It has many flavors.
9. Ice cream can be used for cream in your coffee or tea.

Against:

1. Ice cream has a lot of calories. It makes people fat.
2. Ice cream has sugar and is bad for your teeth.
3. Ice cream goes with many other desserts, and so people just eat too much dessert with ice cream.
4. Ice cream is expensive.
5. All of the toppings just add sugar. You could just eat fruit instead.
6. Some of the flavors of ice cream have more calories than others.
7. People eat all the sugar and get too nervous.
8. Ice cream melts so you can't take it with you anywhere.
9. It costs money to keep the ice cream cold in the freezer.
10. It is very messy, and if you spill you get all sticky.

Additional DEBATE TOPICS to choose.

1. Cell phones in class.... yes and no?
2. School uniforms.... Yes and no?
3. Free public transportation for anyone under 18 years old: yes and no?
4. Students plan lunches at school... yes and no?
5. All the money in the world should be the same currency? yes and no?

Activity #31

DICE ROLL DISCUSSION

Materials: one dice per pair of students, or one large dice for teacher use, list of six topics to discuss on the board or on a handout, list of the words: "who? what? where? when? why? how?" to promote discussion listed on a board or poster, timer.

Skills: speaking, listening, asking questions, describing details

Students pair up. Give each pair a list of six, numbered topics, 1-6. Have them dice role to compete for who rolls first. For example, each rolls once, and the highest number rolled starts. Then, start the timer and yell "Topic" or "Roll em." The first partner rolls and that number is the topic of discussion in English for, say three minutes. During that time, the person who rolled the dice begins the discussion, but either can add to it, and also can ask questions based on the "wh-" questions listed above. The teacher or timer, shouts out "Stop!" or rings a bell or other signal when it is time to switch the topic. Whatever number the dice is, is the topic.

Teacher's note: monitor this closely to make sure that there is discussion in English. Allow for some L1 if the students are beginners. Example topics are: food, traffic, shopping, music, college, people friendly or not, learning a new language, travel.

Activity #32

COMPLIMENTS LINE UP

Materials: board or whiteboard to model a question *Skills: listening, speaking*

Students will line up facing each other in two lines. They will each compliment the person across from them about clothes, hair, friendliness, good English, being nice, being on time for class, etc. After two minutes of talking, one side of the line moves down, and the end person moves over to start again with a new partner.

Before you begin, talk about how to give a compliment. Bring a student to the front of the room to model this with you. On the board or a poster write: "Who?" "What?" "When?" "Where?" "How?" and "Why?" These are excellent prompts for students to inquire of their conversation partner to get more information from them to practice their English speaking and listening skills. Model asking about: clothes, hobbies, favorites, opinions of something, etc.

Variation #1: Students practice saying thank you to their host family, their teacher or a tour guide. Here you want to model what they should say regarding the visit that they have had and thanking the host family or teacher in some specific way.

Activity #33

TRAVEL TALK

Materials: board to model an example *Skills: listening, speaking, asking questions*

Students will line up facing each other in two lines. They will tell their partner across from them about a place that they have visited, one or more things that they liked about it, one or more things that they didn't like, and whether they would return or live there. After 3-5 minutes, students move the line to a new partner. Encourage the use of English at all times if possible.

Activity #34

SHARE ON THE BUS

Materials: microphone *Skills: speaking and listening*

While you tour, you may find yourselves on a bus equipped with a microphone. If you do, you can pass the microphone around for students to share something from their trip, talk about what they did this weekend, what they liked best in class today, their favorite American food, or any of the above. If you'd like, you can list these options on the board before you go, and have them pick one to talk about when they get the microphone. After visiting a location and while returning, you can ask the students to comment on the place they have just been, or ask a question about it using the microphone. On the last day or tour, you could also comment on or thank your group or class.

Variation #1: As the teacher, you can prepare a list of questions to ask students on the way back from a tour. You could present these to them before you go as a scavenger hunt. Give out a prize for the students who get the answer correct.

Activity #35

WHERE WILL YOU BE?

Materials: standard size paper, about 20-25 sheets, markers

Skills: listening, speaking, planning

In this activity students will sit in groups either at tables or on the floor in a circle of about 3 to 5 students per group. Each group will receive a stack of questions on 8-1/2" x 11" paper that has been folded lengthwise with the question written in dark ink on both sides. These then stack on top of each other, and can be removed as the discussion moves forward.

The questions pertain to where the students believe their plans are directed to in the future. Begin with: "What do you think you will be doing in one year? Then advance the question to 2 years, 5 years, 10 years, and 20 years. This is fun because students may plan college, career, marriage, travel, or other surprising things that they think of.

Variation #1: Add in a self-review or a peer-review "How did I do?" that includes how much they think they contributed to the discussion and how well they think they listened to others.

Activity #36

VOCABULARY TOURS

Materials: brochures or prepared text about the tour location that include a vocabulary word bank. *Skills: listening, reading, speaking*

Before you go to a specific site, it is a good idea to help the students understand where they are going, what they will be seeing, and what they will be doing while they are there. You can go to the site or inquire online to find a brochure, or write a modified one for students based on the information provided by the site in English. You can include a vocabulary word bank on your version from which you will ask students to highlight the words that they find in the text.

Variation #1: include a word search puzzle after the reading of the text

Variation #2: make a bingo game (free sites are online for this) using the word bank vocabulary. Divide the class into two teams. Whoever gets the first bingo wins for their team. If it is a tie, then each player has to recite a sentence using one of the bingo words that you select from the tour handout. The sentence with the most words wins. They can compose this as a team if you'd like.

Variation #3: You will read the text about the tour. When students hear a word that is in the word bank, and on the card, they "X" out the bingo word on their card.

Activity #37

ASK A QUESTION

Materials: slips of paper with the instructions to ask a question of someone about a specific topic listed on the paper. *Skills: speaking, reading, listening, connections, vocabulary*

In this activity, the students will practice asking each other at least one question. They should be encouraged to ask additional, extended questions. You can remind them of the "wh-" questions (who, what, where, when, why and how) that help to elicit more information. You can also suggest that they add "Tell me more….when did you…., etc."

Each student receives a slip of paper that directs them to ask a question about a specific topic. They can make the question complicated or simple. Examples for a food-related question might be: what is your favorite American food, or, how do you make "_____" at your house?

They circulate around the room, find a partner, ask each other a question, then switch their pieces of paper and find someone else.

Some topics: American food, host family, travel, school, favorite music, hobbies, pets, family, video games, shopping, learning English, movies, clothes, cooking.

Teacher's note: Allow for some discussion, laughter, and some use of L1, primary language if you would like. Switching the topic papers adds a lot more fun to the activity.

Group table work allows students some time talk in their first language (if you allow) and in English while they collaborate on projects. They can show off their finished project together. If they need help delegating who does what, the teacher can always help with this. Try to be sensitive to who is more outgoing and who might be shy about taking on a speaking role, or a more active role in the group.

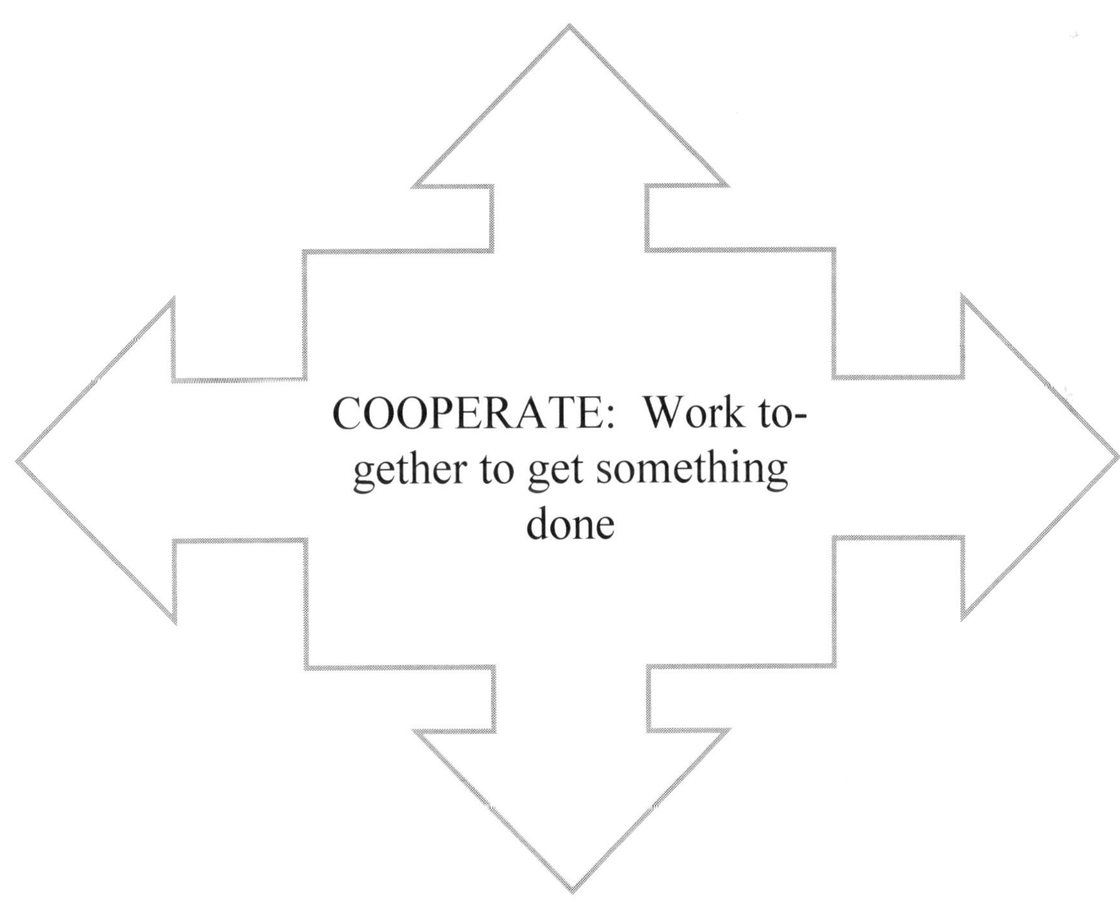

Activity #38

BINGO, WORD SEARCHES and CROSSWORD PUZZLES

Make these related to the tours, field trips, and other outings, grammar points, or vocabulary that your students need to review.

Materials: Bingo sheets, pens or pencils or candy treats for markers, prizes, call sheet.

Skills: *listening, reading, memorization*

There are many online programs that provide free bingo card creators to create your own word cards. There are also creatable word searches and crossword puzzle sites available online.

In the classroom, I sometimes like to ask volunteers to read the bingo words to the class for practice in speaking. Pick a shy student to read the words to the class, and they may not be as shy anymore!

Teacher's note: Ideas for puzzle and game vocabulary are: compound words; topic-specific words such as food, travel, school supplies, clothing, weather, or sports. You can use these activities as a warm-up to a tour you may be going on to help the students become familiar with the vocabulary that they may hear during the tour.

USEFUL HINT: You can also use these to review vocabulary before or after a tour to help students with words they can use in conversation or writing about their day, or to introduce previewing/pre-learning about an upcoming tour.

Activity # 39

DESTINATION DICE a board game that students create themselves

Materials: slips of paper with two boxes on them, large poster paper or cardboard with a blank game board design, dice, markers, pens scissors, glue

Skills: memory, writing, listening, cooperation

Before students go on a tour or visit to say, a museium or a volunteer activity, a movie, a park, etc., give them a paper with a box on it with the following instructions:

While you are on the tour, write down one interesting thing that you saw in the box.

When the students return, have them cut out the papers (which should all be the same size) and glue them onto the poster sized game board, one in each square. Students then team up and take turns rolling dice or choosing spaces from a numbered slip of paper to advance a certain number of spaces until they reach the end and win. You can design the game any way you'd like. The students may want to add pictures, form teams, take turns to roll, and play for their team. The poster can be made from square of paper with different activities written on them by the students. You can play with regular dice, a marker of some kind, and taking turns.

Activity #40

WHERE ON THE MAP?

Materials: Same-sized pieces of paper or index cards, glue, scissors, markers, pencils etc.

Skills: vocabulary, memorization, cooperation, team work

This is a game similar to the one in the previous activity but the students will use a map of a location, such as a college campus or a museum or a shopping mall, or a neighborhood. They can design the game board as they'd like. Include a way to win, either a WIN card or game square for the end, as well as the START.

Students write the locations from the map on the game board squares. They can also make copies to use as cards to put in a stack next to the board.

They take turns picking a card to advance or retreat to a location until they reach the WIN card, or they can roll dice for the number of spaces.

Activity #41

FOOD GROUP POSTER PROJECT

Materials: Flyers of food advertisements from different grocery stores. Poster paper, glue, markers, tables, food groups list (from online or prepare this together).

Skills: Collaboration, teamwork, vocabulary, writing and composition

Many teachers of ESL will take their group on an outing to a grocery store. You can use this outing for a variety of activities, such as a scavenger hunt, or a conversation with a clerk challenge. I had some students who asked people to take their pictures in the store, which was a good conversation and introductory activity.

You can collect a variety of free grocery store ad flyers before your class starts. You can also bring in plastic fruit to study vocabulary and/or pictures of food items.

Directions for students:

(Optional - Today you will make a poster that shows the food groups. Put your names on the poster.) Here students list the five food groups, and can use the ads from grocery stores to determine which food goes into which column.

Then: PLAN A MEAL

Tell the students that it is important to eat three healthy meals every day. Discuss the three meals each day: Ask them when and where they eat each meal.

Breakfast - can be between 6:00 am and 10:00 am

Lunch (or dinner) - can be from 11:00 am to 2:00 pm

Dinner (or supper) - can be from 5:00 pm to 9:00 pm

Your team will plan one meal: either breakfast, lunch, or dinner. List all of the items you will eat, including something to drink and a dessert if you decide to include one. Try to use at least one food from each group. And, remember, it is not good to eat too many sweet foods or desserts!

The students can cut and paste pictures of the items that they choose to prepare for one meal of the day and list the name of the food or include an actual menu list for each meal next to the pictures. Then they can check to see if they have included all the food groups for the day's menu.

Variation #1: After planning the meal, have the students write a grocery list.

Variation #2: Have the students add up the cost of buying the food items from one or more grocery stores.

Activity #42

POSTER DESCRIPTION ART WORK

Materials: markers, colored pencils, poster paper, dictionary

Skills: reading comprehension, collaboration, creativity or imagination

Preface this with talking about describing people. Ask a student to come to the front of the class and use him or her to describe what he looks like and what he is wearing. Talk about age, hair, how tall, thin or not, and clothing.

Hand out poster paper, markers, crayons, rulers, dictionaries if needed. Put students in groups of two or three. Monitor and help with any questions.

Share your art gallery with other classes! Take pictures.

Poster descriptions of people

Directions:

Read the description first. Draw a body like the one on the board and then add to it. Check first to see if you need to pose the arms or legs a certain way.

Description #1: Sam is a student. He has short brown hair with bangs on his forehead. He wears sunglasses. He is trying to grow a beard, so he has some brown hair on his chin. He is smiling because he is happy. He is wearing a red shirt and blue shorts. He is wearing sandals. He has a watch on his left hand. Sam hurt his knee last week, so he has a big beige bandage on his right knee. Sam is walking his little yellow dog, Fluffy. Fluffy is wearing a red collar and a red leash.

Description #2: Jenny is a student. She has long, curly, blonde hair. She looks serious so she is not smiling. She is wearing blue jeans and pink tennis shoes. She is wearing a black jacket. She is going to the library so she is wearing a blue book bag on her left shoulder. She is listening to music, so she has earplugs in her ears.

Description #3: Hana is a student. She has long black hair with bangs on her forehead. She is wearing pink sunglasses that are shaped like squares. She has pink lipstick on but she looks serious. She is wearing a pink and white striped t-shirt with short sleeves and a short, pink skirt. She has long, red socks on and pink sandals with high heels. (She likes pink).

Description #4: Sam is a student. He has short black hair and bangs on his forehead. He is smiling because he is excited about the game. He is wearing a long-sleeved yellow and white striped shirt with a white collar. He has a soccer ball in his right hand (or arm). He is wearing white shorts. He is wearing white short socks and white tennis shoes. He has sunglasses on top of his head. He has a cell phone in his left hand.

Description #5: Jessica is a student. She likes cats. She is wearing a brown t-shirt with short sleeves. She has her cat with her and she is carrying the cat in her arms. She is smiling. She has wearing blue shorts with green tennis shoes and no socks. Jessica has short black hair and bangs on her forehead. She is wearing big hoop (circle) earrings and has a gold necklace around her neck. She has a brown purse on her right shoulder.

Variation #1: Have the handouts ready for each table while you talk about describing people. You could do a matching handout first if your students are beginners, where you match a word with a picture. There are many pictures available online or in magazine that you can use to talk about clothing and to describe people.

Variation #2: Have students pair up describe each other, or go around the room describing to each other. If you are going on tours, try using a place that you have seen together to make a list of describing sentences and a picture about the place, or things that the students remember or did while there.

Activity #43

LETTER TILES TABLE WORK

Materials: letter tiles or small pieces of paper with the letters of the alphabet on them. It is probably better to use lower case letters, in general, to reinforce the visual appearance of English letters and words.

Skills: spelling, vocabulary, cooperation, collaboration

Have some tables set up either in the classroom or in a game or activity center. Set out sets of tiles in sufficient number to allow for playing a game similar to the familiar game of letter tiles many of us have played. Show students how to build words and monitor their progress. This could also be used as a warm-up activity if some students are late getting to class, or at the end of the day to unwind.

Students who attend short-term English programs don't usually expect to find the same types of English language classrooms that they have at their home schools. They expect to become immersed in English language through a variety of activities and practice that may include some experiences with host families and going on tours. However, it is always good to review some basic grammar points that are important to remember when having a conversation with an English speaker.

I generally focus on activities in: basic tense, articles, describing nouns and verbs using adjectives and adverbs, and vocabulary and phrases. Older students may enjoy learning colloquialisms and idioms.

Activity # 44

GREAT TRAVEL DESTINATIONS!

Materials: organizer, pens, pencils *Skills: writing, speaking*

Students will *write* about their travel experience. This is also a great way to prepare for a discussion about travel.

Name ______________________________

The place I really like is….	The best thing about it is…..

Some really fun things to do there are…..

Fun things to do	But, one thing I didn't like was…….
1. 2. 3. 4. 5.	

Variation #1: Students can exchange and read to the class to guess who wrote it.

Variation #2: Pair the students at their table and have them exchange and read to each other.

Variation #3: Students exchange and read each other's aloud to the class.

Activity #45

WORD CONNOTATIONS or *Shades of Meaning*

Materials: paper, handout

Skills: listening, speaking, vocabulary, grammar

Shades of Meaning

When we have a conversation or write an essay, we like to add words that give our message extra meaning. We like to use describing words.

When describing a noun, we usually will use an adjective. We say that something or someone, or an idea *is, was* or *will be* _____ (describing word.) This is called the predicate adjective.

For example: My teacher is happy. The word "happy" describes the teacher.

Or My teacher will be angry. The word "angry" also describes the teacher.

Most of us want a "happy" teacher. We see "happy" as a positive, good word to describe someone. "Angry" is a negative, not-so-good word to describe our teacher.

We use these descriptive words to sound more interesting when we talk and write about topics.

Read the words below. After you read them, sort them by **positive** or **negative** in meaning, as best you can.

Remember these words are used to describe a person, place, thing or an idea.

confident

extravagant

steep

specific

lonesome

prominent

Sort the words	
GOOD MEANING (Positive)	BAD MEANING (Negative)

Now we will use some new words in a sentence. Read the clue below the blank and then pick a word that fits into the sentence. You can work with a partner.

Word Bank
steep prominent specific lonesome extravagant confident

1. The tour was about a ____________________ site in the city.
(easy to see, stands out)
2. We climbed some really __________________ hills on our hike.
(hard to climb, straight up)
3. The clerk told me that only __________________ items were on sale today.
(certain, only some)
4. When I leave my cat at home all day, I think he must get very __________________. (lonely, all by himself)
5. The host family prepared an ______________ meal. (special, expensive)
6. The student was very ______________ when he gave his speech. (not nervous)

To Teacher: Lastly, provide new words in a hat or bowl or bag. Ask the students to pick one of them and decide on their own what kind of meaning the word has. They then can talk or write about a specific topic, perhaps a favorite vacation spot, person, or a shopping experience using the word that they have selected in a sentence. Have them work with a partner, who then gives his or her best interpretation of the word *meaning*. They can work together to look up the words in an online dictionary or thesaurus. Provide writing paper.

Examples:

generous	inaccurate	expensive	cheap
valuable	inspiring	famous	risky
difficult	appetizing	boring	enthusiastic
reliable	careful	rude	engaging

Teacher's note: You can always add or change these words to match any other activities you may be doing, or to challenge your learners.

Activity #46

ARTICLES "a" "an" and "the"

Materials: board or whiteboard, realia, short story or article

Skills: listening, reading, team work, giving feedback

Many languages do not use the articles "a" "an" and "the." Therefore, it is a good idea to review the use of these three useful words with your summer learners. The reason for this is simple. The English that they do know and practice while they are here will sound much better if they can incorporate these articles into their speech as much as possible. For example: "We went to Space Needle today. " "We went to <u>the</u> Space Needle today."

The rules are simple to explain and to provide examples of. First, make sure that the students know the letters of the alphabet. Sometimes I print these out in large letters and put them up at the front of the room. Review the difference between consonants and vowels. Write some nouns that start with each. Review what a noun is. Remind students that if a noun begins with a vowel, use "an." If the noun starts with a consonant, use "a." Have a list of nouns ready and practice as a whole class using "a" or "an."

For use of "the" article: Remind the students "the" is an indefinite article by having some realia or photos available. For example: from a stand of <u>chocolate bars</u>, you would select **a** chocolate <u>b</u>ar. If there is only one chocolate bar on **the** <u>table</u> and you eat it – you ate "**the**" <u>chocolate bar</u>.

Do a choral reading of this skit:

*For lunch today we went to **the** cafeteria. I ate **an** apple, **an** egg and **a** slice of pizza. It was **the** best lunch.*

*For lunch yesterday we went to **a** bad restaurant. I ate **a** salad, **an** egg sandwich and **a** piece of pie. I got sick. It was **the** worst lunch. Or…*

*We went on **a** boat ride. We sailed up and down **the** Sound for **an** hour. (Silent [h]). **The** weather was good. By **the** time we got to **the** bus to go back, it started to rain. No one had **an** umbrella.*

When you provide these examples to the students, whether on a board, poster, or on a paper for each student to keep, check for understanding by asking them to tell you what they know the pattern to be after you have reviewed, explained and practiced. If they are still uncertain, just review again. Hearing and practicing speaking with and without articles also helps to reinforce the correct sound of the sentence pattern.

Variation #1: Hand out a short article or a short story, pair the students, and have them highlight or circle or underline the articles and then read the story to each other.

Variation #2: After the students read the article or short story and highlight all of the articles, divide the class into three groups. One group is the article "a", the second is the article "an", and the third is the article "the." As you read, the groups will raise their hand when they hear the article assigned to their group. This is a good opportunity to provide some feedback and review on the rules that apply.

Activity #47

TENSE TIME LINE

Materials: masking or freezer tape, list of statements that utilize present, past and future statements. These can be varied in difficulty depending upon the proficiency of the student.

Skills: teamwork, listening, practice toward writing

Review of: Simple past, simple present and future tense.

There are many creative and fun ways to practice the simple tenses.

Divide the students into two teams and have them line up. Place a long piece or pieces of masking tape on the floor where there is plenty of space. This is your timeline. Label the middle section as "present," the farthest section to the left side as facing as "past," and the farthest section to the right side as "future."

Next, the teacher or a student reads statements one at a time and the students from each team will select their spot on the timeline. Leave room for two students as both may get the correct answer and need to stand in the same location. Keep score on their responses.

Variation #1: Have each team write some sentences for the other team to answer.

Variation #2: Make this theme-related. Use a theme such as a sport, shopping, travel, cooking or school to help the students stay focused on the topic and help them process the language.

Shopping theme tense timeline sentences:

1. I want to go shopping this afternoon. (future)
2. I went to the store to buy some fruit. (past)
3. I am shopping at the store for some dinner. (present) etc.
4. Do you shop at the store on the corner?
5. There is a sale at the mall.
6. I bought some shoes and a dress.
7. I paid a lot of money for my souvenirs.
8. It costs $20.00 to get into the Space Needle.
9. I am going to go to a movie tomorrow with my friends.
10. We had a nice time at your house.

Eating out theme tense timeline sentences:

1. The food here is delicious!
2. Did you like the steak you ate here last time?
3. I am eating a salad tonight.
4. There is a fly in my soup!
5. I need some more water.
6. I ordered the cake, but I got pie.
7. We should go there again soon.
8. Let me pay for your dinner, please.
9. Did you have the chicken or the fish?
10. How much tip should I give the waiter?

Activity #48

ROUND ROBIN PHONICS

Materials: phonics cards with up to five words that contain the same phonics sound, envelopes or bags and markers, tokens such as pennies, small candy, buttons, stickers, erasers, stamps, etc., a timer. *Skills: pronunciation, listening – good for beginners.*

This is set up like a jigsaw game, where each person in a team has a phonics card with up to five words that focus on the same phonics practice for each word and the phonics "sound" listed on the other side. Divide the students into two teams. The goal is to get around the room as quickly as possible, collecting a token at each station that the player gets the focus phonics sound correct. The player with the most tokens at the end is the winner. You can give the students an envelope or a small plastic bag that they can write their name on to put the tokens in as they go. If there is a tie, you will need some extra "bonus/tie-breaker" challenge phonics cards. You can make these as challenging as you'd like and could include a performance activity such as using the words on the cards in a sentence within a certain amount of time. Each team should get a specified amount of time for all members to go around the room and collect tokens.

Some example include: the "wh-" sound, as in: which, what, when, where, whale; "bl-"sound, as in: black, block, blank, blue; "sh-" sound, as in: shirt, shut, shout; "ch-" sound, as in: change, church, chop, chance; etc. Be sure when you make your cards that you indicate on the other side what the phonics focus is. This way, players support each other in the learning process.

Students with cards make stations around the room in a circle. This is Team A. Team B will go around to each station as quickly as possible, reading the words and giving the Team A player their answer. If correct, they get a token. They count their tokens. The players with the most are the winners. Then the teams switch and Team B exhibits their phonics cards. Each team should have a different set of cards and sounds. Be sure to give each team the same amount of time to play. Then the bonus challenge round.

Activity #49

TOPIC (or HOT) SEAT

Materials: one chair, a whiteboard or chalkboard or poster paper and markers or chalk, and an imagination!
Skills: speaking, listening, explaining, creativity, cooperation

This game is really fun, and can be used with any topic. One student sits in a chair in front of the room with his or her back to the board or poster. Another student writes a word from a category on the board or poster paper behind the student, who cannot see the word. The topic is shared with all students. The class provides clues that do not include the actual word, or the name of the word or object, but not using the specific word that is listed on the board. The student who is seated must try to guess the word. When he or she guesses correctly, you can add a point for the team, and allow the student to chose the next hot seat student, and to write a new word on the board/poster. Some example topics: school supplies, hobbies, food, places to visit, countries, capitols, famous landmarks, movies, toys or games, books, careers, clothing.

Activity #50

VOCABULARY LABELS IN THE ROOM (Good for beginning learners)

Materials: labels or sticky notes, list of items for each team

Skills: vocabulary, team work

Label several objects in the room with sticky notes. Divide into two teams. Give each team a list of the names of the same objects in the classroom that have labels on them. Start the timer. Students race to collect the most sticky notes that match their list. The team that gets the most correctly matched labels collected in three minutes wins.

Bring in boxes of crayons with the basic colors easy to read on the labels. Have the students each pick a color and a piece of paper. Have them go around the room finding things that are the same color and write down the name of what they found in English with the crayon.

Activity #51

NOUNS AND ADJECTIVES BALL TOSS

Materials: inflatable ball or stuffed animal toy, whiteboard or poster board or black board.

Skills: parts of speech, speaking, cooperation

Write a simple explanation of what a noun is on the board or poster paper. List as: person, place or thing (and idea/concept) in column headings. Provide a couple of examples of each, then have the students call out some more nouns to add to the columns.

Next, review what an adjective is: words that describe nouns. Write one of the nouns on the poster such as "car" and have the students help you brainstorm some adjectives for "car," such as shiny, new, old, fast, etc.

Next, start the ball toss by picking a noun, toss the ball or toy to someone who then has to use a describing word that fits the noun. Then that person tosses the ball to another player and selects a noun her or she must describe using an adjective.

Activity #52

WORD WEB TOPICS

Materials: markers or erase board markers, poster paper or lots of white board or chalk board space and chalk

Skills: vocabulary, word associations, teamwork

This is the word web example for the activity. Model the activity by putting the word "beach" or other theme word as a location in the center. Then include the other words in bubbles with lines attached.

Where are we going? To the beach! Beach will be the center word. Around "Beach" will be other words associated with the beach. Categorize examples as following: *Noises – happy people, dogs, loud Nature – wind, sun, ocean, sand, waves Food*

- *BBQ, drinks, ice cream,* Word Web categories continued…*etc. Parking lot – cars, buses, walking with sand in your shoes Picnic - Chairs, tables, benches Beach – lawn chairs, blankets, swim suits, suntan lotion, waves, sand, wet dogs, hot sun, life-guard, suntan Park – games, frisbee games, games in the water, surfing Sharks? Continue to sort by category.*

Examples to start:

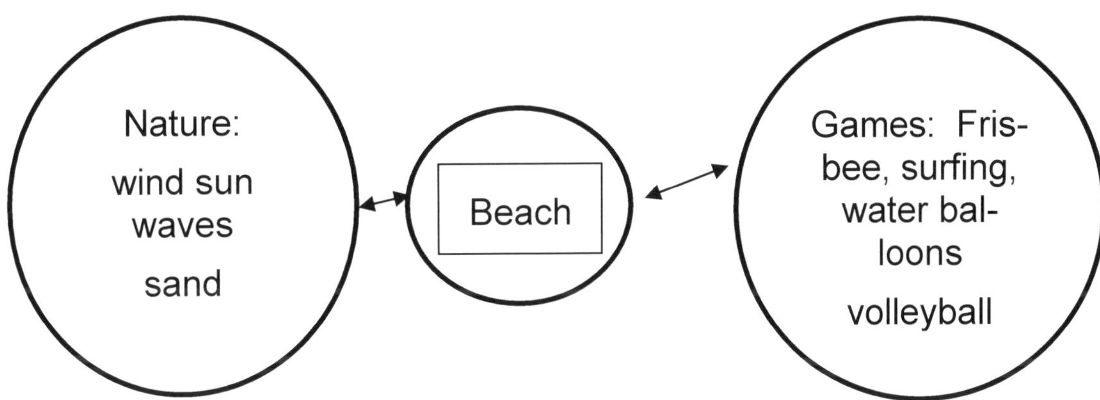

Keep adding bubbles with categories related vocabulary in each bubble. Use this to get your students started on a writing activity.

Activity #53

READING FOR GIST

Materials: short newspaper or online article that is age appropriate and at about the right level for the learners, or just a bit more difficult. List of vocabulary for each article if needed. Poster paper, markers, example poster

Skills: reading, collaboration, presentation, speaking

Divide the students into teams of 3-4 each team. Give each team an article to read. They should each have a copy to read individually as well as together. Give them an organizer that asks them to find the main idea and three interesting details about the article. They decide on a writer/dictation taker. Once they have finished the organizer, they will transfer that information onto a poster, add a drawing if they wish, or anything else to help them make their presentation.

Then each group will read their article (one person reads, or they split the reading) and present their details. They can decide who will read the article and who will read the main idea/details and who will explain any drawings, for example.

Activity #54

STORY SEQUENCE RACE

Materials: a well-written, age and level appropriate short story of about 5-7 lines. Paper and pencils/pens, tape.

Skills: reading vocabulary and comprehension, sequencing, memory, writing, collaboration

Compose or locate an appropriate story or short news article. Break the article/story down into one sentence each on separate pieces of paper that you will tape around the room, but not in a sequential order. Pair the students in twos. One student will go around the room, memorize one sentence, bring it back to the scribing student at the table, and dictate the sentence to him or her.

When all of the sentences have been dictated, the pair will sit down and order them correctly in sequence to make the story or item readable and understandable. The first team to finish and do it correctly wins. Be sure to keep a copy of the original for yourself.

Variation #1: When you have found a winner, then have students sequentially order the paragraph with either: first, next, then, next, and last; or, 1st, 2nd, 3rd, etc.

Variation #2: Prior to teaching this activity, teach the ordinal numbers by giving each student an ordinal number on a piece of paper. Then have students come up to the front, line up correctly, and read off their number.

Variation #3: Model how to sequence by asking the students to watch you: open the door, enter the room, say hello, put down your folders, get students' attention, and begin working. Then ask them to recite back what you did first, second, and/or then, next, etc., and finally, or last.

Activity #55

CREATE A SENTENCE – BUILD A STORY

Materials: Sentences that have been clipped into one-word pieces, one sentence for each group, board, marker or chalk

Skills: Writing strategies, grammar and syntax, collaboration, speaking and listening in discussion format

Divide the students into as many groups as you will have in your finished product; for example, four groups, one sentence for each group, for four sentences total. Type up or write the sentence in somewhat larger letters, then cut them into pieces, one word each piece. Paper clip them together and give one set or sentence to each group. They will order the words into a complete sentence. Then, each group will dictate their completed sentences to the teacher or a student scribe, who will write the sentence on the board. Lastly, the works together to put them in order.

Activity #56

LETTER TILES TABLE WORK

Materials: letter tiles or small pieces of paper with the letters of the alphabet on them. It is probably better to use lower case letters, in general, to reinforce the visual appearance of English letters and words.

Skills: spelling, vocabulary, cooperation, collaboration

Have some tables set up either in the classroom or in a game or activity center. Set out sets of tiles in sufficient number to allow for playing a game similar to the familiar game of letter tiles many of us have played. Show the students how to build words and monitor their progress. This could also be used as a warm-up activity if some students are late getting to class, or at the end of the day to unwind.

Activity #57

CONCENTRATION CARDS

Materials: Provide sets of made-up or manufactured words in some category or pattern that you want to practice, scissors, markers. *Skills: memorization, vocabulary, cooper-ation*

Make two of each type of card, then give one set to each table. Students place all of the cards face down, and then take turns trying to match. If they don't match, they turn the cards back to face-down and wait for the next turn. You can easily make written verb tense cards using index cards. You will also need scissors and markers.

Variation #1: Include anything on the cards that you want your students to work with or practice. You could include idioms, money, holidays, tourist sites, grammar rules, food, parts of speech, or cities or countries, for example. You may also want to match pictures with the noun or verb that may describe the person, place, thing or action.

Activity #58

VOCABULARY MATCHING GALLERY

Materials: poster paper, pictures and matching vocabulary words, glue or tape, scissors

Skills: basic vocabulary, speaking, listening, collaboration, giving feedback or corrections

Students create a poster of pictures that you have drawn (or printed from online for students to use) to match vocabulary with words by placing them on the poster next to the corresponding picture. Divide the students into 3 or 4 teams. Provide the poster paper with the pictures neatly lined up with space next to them for the words; or, you can let the students match and tape or glue the words and pictures onto poster paper together as a group. When done, have them sign names and put them up for a gallery walk around the room. Monitor work and check it when done. Watch for mistakes, and lead them to correct the errors in positive ways.

Some examples would be:

picture: (it is) raining

picture: (he is) running

picture: (they are) eating

picture: (the season) winter, fall, spring, etc.

picture: school, bus stop, cinema, shopping mall, etc.

Activity #59

WORD ORDER LINE UP

Materials: individual pages with words of a sentence on them.

Skills: cooperation, sentence structure, reading, speaking

Divide the class into 2-3 teams, depending upon the number of students that you have. Give each of your teams a set of pages with individual words on them that make a sentence. Have them each line up holding the word in front of them to make the sentence. Have each team present their sentence separately to the class, and have the rest of the class peer review, making changes if necessary and providing an explanation for the adjustment or change.

Activity #60

TOUR GUIDE

Materials: the following chart in the form of a handout, list of site specific vocabulary words, pens, pencils, translators or a dictionary.

Skills: vocabulary, writing, categorizing details, summarizing

Here the students will act as a tour guide and use the organizer to list some points about a place that they have been. In one class, we played "Hot Seat" (previously listed in Chapter Four) before this activity. We also had a map of the world and located where we had been with markers.

TOUR GUIDE Handout

<table>
<tr><td colspan="3">Name ______________ Date ___________Location_____________________</td></tr>
<tr><td colspan="3"><u>Word Bank</u>
Here you will list words that you have studied or will be using during the tour. Use no more than 10, site-specific, new or review vocabulary. You may have used these same words in another activity such as bingo or a writing activity.</td></tr>
<tr><td>Where did you go for your tour?</td><td>Who was there?</td><td>What did you see?</td></tr>
<tr><td>When did you go?</td><td>Why did you go to visit this place?</td><td>How did you like the tour?</td></tr>
<tr><td colspan="3">List three words from the word bank that you remember from the tour.</td></tr>
<tr><td>1.</td><td>2.</td><td>3.</td></tr>
<tr><td colspan="3">Write three complete sentences about the tour using the three words.</td></tr>
<tr><td colspan="3">1.

2.

3.</td></tr>
</table>

This activity gets the students ready to do some more in-depth writing about their visit to the country. Allow use of translators or a dictionary. It is probably a good idea to make this independent work, rather than group work. This can be assigned as home-work.

Activity #61

LISTEN AND WRITE

Materials: CD player, or computer with speakers, a copy of the lyrics for teacher, a set of lyrics with some "close" or fill in the blank lines from the song.

Skills: listening, writing

This is a listening cloze activity where the teacher plays a popular song and students supply missing words from written lyrics as they listen. They will listen once, then get a paper from you with the lyrics with some blanks with missing words. You will play the song at least once more, or perhaps two more times, allowing the students to com-plete the paper.

Variation #1: Play the song once, divide the group into two teams, play the song again, and have teams sing the designated word that is missing on their lyrics close handout.

Variation #2: Pre-teach the vocabulary that you want to focus on, or perhaps a grammar point that you might want to use as the "cloze" or "blank missing word(s).

Activity #62

WRITING A POST CARD

Students like to collect souvenirs of their visits, and postcards are inexpensive and descriptive of locations that they have toured.

Materials: large poster paper or whiteboard, markers, sample post card organizer for students, real post cards for them to keep *Skills: reading, writing, dictation*

You can model how to write a post card by making a large-sized poster of a post card and have the students dictate an example writing to parents or a friend.

Read a few sample postcard "scripts" that you composed or find online as examples first. Such as:"Dear mom and dad, I am having a good time in the US. Today we went to a park and played games.

People here are really nice. I am making new friends. I like my teacher. I miss you. Love, Student."

You may want to "make up" a picture or site that you visited for the other side of the post card. It is important that they understand where to put the text they are writing, and where the address should be. Make sure that they understand that, if you do give them an actual post card, they do not need to send it in the mail and can just take it home with them. Or, you can buy stamps and mail the cards for your students.

Variation: For one class that I had, I printed color pictures of sites from our area and the students cut them out and glued them onto computer-generated postcards that I had printed out for practice.

Activity #63

THANK YOU CARDS

Materials: colored paper, heavy duty poster paper, scissors, glue, stickers, ribbon, etc., markers, colored pencils, tape, ribbons

Skills: imagination, artistic, appreciative wording

Students can make their own thank you cards for their host families or for their teacher, or tour guides, or whomever you feel deserves a thanks from them. Before you start, give them some vocabulary and complete but short ways to thank the person(s) that fit the situation. Give the cards time for the glue to dry.

Activity #64

FINAL WRITING OR PRESENTATION

Materials: paper, pencils, pen, organizers for writing, dictionary, exemplars, notecards, markers, audio and/or video recording capability if desired

Skills: writing, organizing, editing, speaking and presenting

Schools who send groups of students to study in another country sometimes send along the English teacher from the school that the students attend. This teacher will collaborate with you, and may translate some of your lessons if needed. It is important that you help them to feel comfortable and needed, but, since they don't have your lesson plans unless you give them your plans, you will need to decide how to best handle their presence in your classroom. I feel comfortable with the teacher observing, monitoring students, helping when needed, and taking over when giving directions for outside activities or extra assignments on their own agenda.

One such assignment may be a writing task, such as writing about themselves, their future plans, past accomplishments or writing about their visit. Depending upon the students' levels and the teacher's expectations, the assignment may or may not include a presentation, or even a contest for prizes.

If the students are writing during class times, or writing at home and editing during class, it is important that you provide some support to this task. It is good to be available to help plan the writing including selecting topics, and to help edit, review, and listen to speeches if you are able and have time.

I would provide an organizer for the writing assignment, discuss length, length of a speaking presentation if required, and provide dictionaries and translation through mobile phones or other online tools if possible.

An organizer would contain sections to jot down: 1) main idea or topic, 2) a thesis or opening statement, 3) at least three sections to list three important details, and 4) a section to draft a closing statement.

The steps in the writing process include: 1) prewrite including planning with organizers, 2) writing, which involves composing ideas in complete sentences around your topic and details, 3) revision, which can include teacher comments and peer editing/comments, 4) student incorporates suggested and needed changes, and, 5) publishing or final copy for presentation or submission for final comments

Teachers may wish to review some writing expectations prior to the start of the writing task through providing example sentences on the board or in a handout. Consider the following qualities of good writing:

1) ideas or themes or topics,

2) personal tone of the writer's message,

3) vocabulary a writer chooses to convey meaning,

4) rhythm and flow of the language,

5) mechanical correctness, and,

6) organization and how the document appears visually and what format is it in (Power Point, pictorial, hand written or typed, or other).

If you have an exact assignment for the students, consider providing them with an actual essay to read through and model theirs from. This is helpful for them to notice things such as vocabulary, punctuation, parallelism, subject/verb agreement, format and fluency.

Variation #1: self-review or peer review exit ticket

When teaching, remember to give any handouts to each student to put in a folder. Many programs have a check-in with the school English teacher at home, who will want to see what the students were working on in the class. Also, parents will want to know what their student has learned. And, of course, the students will want memories and souvenirs of their visit.

Error correction for any students should be done with the best intentions. These include: keeping the students level of self-confidence high, not embarrassing or making fun of the student or the error, giving reasons why the correction is needed, and modeling using examples. Lastly, practice should be provided at some point for the whole class, since any mistake that one student may make, could also be a mistake that other's might make.

TO BOLDLY GO WHERE MAKING A MISTAKE IS OK!

Activity #65

CORRECTING WITH KINDNESS

When giving feedback or corrections, try to follow a consistent pattern.

1) Acknowledgement of the error and the intended statement meaning.
2) Paraphrase, or state what you think the student might have meant.
3) Kindly offer a suggested grammar point to consider (tense, pronouns use, plurals, parallelism, subject/verb agreement, etc.)
4) Give the student a chance to fix the error.
5) Help if needed.
6) Give praise for correct answer.
7) Practice examples for retention.

Activity #66

LISTEN UP – Listening Corrections

Materials: none *Skills: listening, speaking, grammar, collaboration*

Have your students focus their attention on your speaking voice as you state the following sentences. You will work with the students to correct the spoken errors, and to restate the sentence with the corrections. Some sentences may require reordering the phrases or clauses as you make corrections. Finally, give each group or table a "problem" sentence and ask them to practice saying it aloud. They will then make note of what needs to be corrected within the sentence. Then, they will chose one person to restate the sentence as they have corrected it.

#1. "I have many good times while I was in Seattle."

Hints:

1. This sentence has an error in verb tense
2. The tense should be in the past
3. "had" not "have"

#2. "We saw a lot of different kind of people's car here."

Hints:

1. The error is with the nouns
2. The error involves count or non count nouns
3. An "s" needs to be added to "kinds" and "cars" kinds is a variety or type of car (there are many here); and car is a count nouns and requires an "s" to make it plural

#3. The food is very good we had at restaurant.

Hints:

1. The error is in the tense of the verb "is" (should be past tense "was")
2. The word "restaurant" requires an article "the"
3. This sentence also requires a relative pronoun to describe the antecedent "food."
   So, the sentence should read: "The food that we had at the Restaurant was very good."

Following these examples, or other common errors that you hear while working with your students, create a sentence for each group that allows them work together to fix the errors. Try to keep the errors similar to the ones that you have already modeled or demonstrated correcting in class. This way, they can gain confidence in the grammar rules. Once the groups present their sentence and why made any changes from the original, you can work with the whole class to agree or disagree, or make additional changes. The most difficult part in this is that you are not to write anything down, even on the board! It's all listening, speaking and working through the challenges.

Variation #1: I would encourage each person in the group to practice speaking the sentence while the students are working, both before and after corrections are made.

Activity #67

WHAT I THINK ABOUT WHAT YOU SAID - Peer review of student presentations.

Materials: Handouts, student presentation *Skills: listening, speaking,, communicating ideas*

Sometimes students in short-term programs are required by their teachers to present at the end of the session. While teachers may know what to look for and to listen for in a student's speech, often times the students are a little uncertain. This is where a rubric comes in handy for the teachers or judges. However, the students can have a kind of a rubric through the use of a peer review checklist.

By handing this out during practice sessions, students can read the anonymous peer reviews and make changes that their classmates think would make their presentations more effective.

Peer Review

<table>
<tr><td colspan="3">Speaker ______________________ Date ____________________
Topic:</td></tr>
<tr><td>Was the speech interesting?</td><td>Could you hear the speaker?</td><td>Was this helpful or informative?</td></tr>
<tr><td>YES NO</td><td>YES NO</td><td>YES NO</td></tr>
<tr><td colspan="3">Are there any changes that you would suggest?

Do not sign your name! Return this form to the teacher. Thank you!</td></tr>
</table>

Activity 68

A REVIEW FOR YOU

Peer review for more advanced presentations classes. This form gives the students more flexibility in their comments, which can actually be very helpful to the teacher, and may help to inform instruction in your classrooms.

Presenters: ______________________________ Date: _______________

Subject of the presentation: ______________________________________

FOCUS: What is the speaker's connection with the topic? How is he or she involved?

What details does the speaker include to tell you about or about his or her experience?

1.
2.
3.

What is good about the presentation?

How could the speaker make this a better presentation?

Do not include your name. Please return this form to the teacher.

Activity #69

COMMENT SHEET

This is a very flexible comment sheet that lets students write nearly any type of comments that they feel may be helpful. Again, request that these be anonymous. Most students are not unkind in their reviews, but this form allows for some ambiguity, and just asks for the listener's viewpoint on the presentation.

Speaker ________________________ Date _________________________

Title or Topic: ____

Response/Comment	Why I think this will help.

Activity #70

CHAT FOR 3 – Conversation Participation Self Review Checklist

In this activity, students will track and rate themselves on their own conversational skills by logging who they spoke to, what they discussed and some details that were included in the conversation. Arrange chairs in a circle or find a large room to move around in. Students will circulate while you play some music for one minute. Then they will have 3 minutes each to talk to the person they have selected or who is sitting to their right or left (you chose). Each student has a tracking "Self-Review Checklist" as below to complete.

Materials: handouts, chairs or a large area to move around in, cell phone with music or CD player.

Skills: listening and speaking

Continued on next page.

If you'd like to give out prizes for the ones that are completed fully, that is even better!

CHAT FOR 3

My name: ______________________________ Date: ______________________

Topic: (Examples) Field Trip, My Hobbies, Travel Experiences, etc. (You can chose or the students can chose on their own during the one minute music break.)

I talked to:

1. ______________ 2. ___________________ 3. _________________

3 things I mentioned	3 things I mentioned	3 things I mentioned

---

3 things they mentioned	3 things they mentioned	3 things they mentioned

GOODBYES and WHAT TO TAKE HOME FROM CLASS FOR SHORT STAY PROGRAMS STUDENTS

Materials: Folders for each student, stickers, markers

Skills: ongoing practice, sharing of experiences

I usually give each student a folder to take home with them. If you recall, we decorated these at the beginning of the class/book. I remind them as we work to put their papers into the folder. This can be shared with parents and teachers when they get home.

If you'd like, make them a small packet to take on the plane with some crossword puzzles, word searches, or articles on the sites that they have seen to read on the plane, and to share when they get home. For one class, I made up a short story with jumbled sentences and online pictures to work on during their trip home.

Despite some teary-eyed goodbyes, remember the students will likely be very happy once they've arrived home.

Natalie Johnson is a teacher of English Language Learners in Washington State and in the State of Minnesota. She holds a Master of Arts in ELL K-12, and a Cambridge University, UK, CELTA. She also holds a Master of Science in Education in Reading. Ms. Johnson is currently pursuing a Master of Arts in English Teaching Secondary.

For a printable copy of organizers from the text for classroom use, please visit:

https://www.teacherspayteachers.com/

Search: "ESL Activities for the Classroom Organizers" to purchase all of the organizers from the text for $3.00 US. They do accept PayPal.

Zeitfracht Medien GmbH
Ferdinand-Jühlke-Straße 7
99095 Erfurt, Deutschland
produktsicherheit@kolibri360.de